Rey Mysterio®

Written by Kevin Sullivan

DK Publishing

Rey Mysterio is one of WWE's best-known Superstars. He has won nearly every honor sports-entertainment has to offer, including the World Championship. However, despite all the success he has today, becoming one of the greatest wasn't an easy task for Mysterio.

Rey Mysterio's Stats
- **Height:** 5' 6" (1.68 m)
- **Weight:** 175 lbs. (79 kg)
- **Hometown:** San Diego, CA
- **Signature Moves:** 619, West Coast Pop

Mysterio's career began in 1989. Standing just 5' 6" (1.68 m), many thought his much larger opponents would crush him. Thanks to the training he received from his uncle, legendary Mexican wrestler Rey Misterio, Sr., the small Superstar became a big hit.

REY MYSTERIO, JR.
FLYINGFURY

WCW
MONDAY
NITRO
TNT
THE RULES HAVE CHANGED

After several years competing in
Mexico, Mysterio moved to the United
States where he began competing for
Philadelphia's ECW in 1995. He wasn't
there very long before his high-flying
moves caught the eyes of WCW.
They signed him to a contract in 1996.

As a member of WCW, Mysterio finally got the chance to compete under the national spotlight. With millions of fans watching his every move, he climbed to the top of the cruiserweight division. He even won the Cruiserweight Championship five different times.

Rey Mysterio's lightning-fast moves made him one of WCW's most popular Superstars. Even though he had millions of fans, he never reached main-event status. It wasn't until 2002, when Mysterio joined WWE, that his full potential became apparent.

Only one month into his WWE career, Mysterio targeted one of *SmackDown*'s best Superstars when he challenged Kurt Angle to a match at *SummerSlam*. It was Mysterio's biggest match of his career. Unfortunately, he lost the contest to Angle.

However, he soon got his revenge when he teamed with Edge to beat Angle and his partner for the WWE Tag Team Championship in November 2002. The win gave Mysterio his first taste of gold in WWE, but it wasn't his last. Over the next several years, Mysterio would go on to win many more championships.

After his WWE Tag Team Championship reign, Mysterio focused his attention on the Cruiserweight Title. He held the title five times with WCW, but never as a member of WWE. In June 2003, he finally accomplished his goal when he beat Matt Hardy for the gold on *SmackDown*.

Over the next year, Mysterio went on to win the Cruiserweight Championship two more times. He beat Tajiri in January 2004 and Chavo Classic several months later. His victory over Chavo gave Mysterio his eighth Cruiserweight Championship. No other Superstar held the title more times.

Rey Mysterio's Cruiserweight Championship Victories

1. Rey Mysterio beat Dean Malenko: July 8, 1996

2. Rey Mysterio beat Eddie Guerrero: October 26, 1997

3. Rey Mysterio beat Juventud Guerrera: January 15, 1998

4. Rey Mysterio beat Billy Kidman: March 15, 1999

5. Rey Mysterio beat Psychosis: April 26, 1999

6. Rey Mysterio beat Matt Hardy: June 5, 2003

7. Rey Mysterio beat Tajiri: January 1, 2004

8. Rey Mysterio beat Chavo Classic: June 17, 2004

Over the course of his career, Rey Mysterio had a very close friendship with Eddie Guerrero. Their relationship seemed to become even stronger in February 2005 when the two Superstars teamed to beat the Basham Brothers for the WWE Tag Team Championship. However, their friendship soon ended when Guerrero turned on Mysterio.

The former buddies competed in several matches over the next few months. Mysterio won every time, which bothered Guerrero greatly. Finally, an upset Guerrero tried to get under his rival's skin by claiming he was the true father of Mysterio's son, Dominic.

The two Superstars decided to settle their differences in a Ladder Match at *SummerSlam*. The winner of the match would be awarded full custody of Dominic. Fighting for his family's honor, Mysterio climbed to the top of the ladder first and won the match.

Not many people thought Rey Mysterio could win the 2006 *Royal Rumble*. They said he was too small to beat Big Show, Triple H, Viscera, Kane, and all the other giants competing in the match. In the end, the "Ultimate Underdog" proved his greatness by tossing Randy Orton over the top rope to win the event.

Mysterio's *Royal Rumble* victory awarded him a chance at the World Championship at *WrestleMania 22*. He battled Kurt Angle and Randy Orton in a Triple Threat Match that night. Once again, few gave Mysterio a chance to win. He proved everyone wrong when he pinned Orton to become World Champion. Finally, after 15 years in the ring, Mysterio had won the big one.

Mysterio held the title for four months before losing it to King Booker at *The Great American Bash*. During the match, Mysterio's friend Chavo Guerrero turned on him by helping Booker win. This set up another great Mysterio-Guerrero rivalry. This time, Chavo injured Mysterio so badly that he needed surgery on his knee.

Rey Mysterio was out of action for almost one full year. He finally returned to the ring at *SummerSlam* where beat Chavo Guerrero. The win didn't give Mysterio any titles. However, it was just as rewarding as a championship victory, because he won revenge from the Superstar who injured him.

Unfortunately for Mysterio, his comeback didn't last very long. Just a few short months later, he seriously injured his arm. He needed several surgeries to repair the injury. Mysterio could not compete for more than four months.

When Rey Mysterio returned to the ring, he was quickly drafted from *SmackDown* to *Raw.* The change in shows didn't slow down the high-flyer at all. He picked up big wins over such Superstars as Kane, Kofi Kingston, and The Miz.

Rey Mysterio's *WrestleMania* Matches

WrestleMania XIX:
Rey Mysterio lost to Matt Hardy, Cruiserweight Championship

WrestleMania XX:
10-Man Cruiserweight Open

WrestleMania 21:
Rey Mysterio beat Eddie Guerrero

However, his biggest victory as a member of the *Raw* roster came when he beat JBL in less than one minute to capture the Intercontinental Championship at *WrestleMania XXV.*

WrestleMania 22:
Rey Mysterio beat Kurt Angle and Randy Orton, World Championship

WrestleMania XXV:
Rey Mysterio beat JBL, Intercontinental Championship

WrestleMania XXVI:
Rey Mysterio beat CM Punk

Rey Mysterio was drafted back to *SmackDown* after *WrestleMania XXV*. He took his Intercontinental Championship with him, but lost it to Chris Jericho shortly after arriving. Over the next several weeks, the two Superstars competed in many matches, including a Steel Cage Match.

Finally, in late June 2009, Mysterio beat Jericho in a Title vs. Mask Match at *The Bash* to reclaim the Intercontinental Championship.

Mysterio defended his second Intercontinental Title against the mighty Kane, Dolph Ziggler, and others for more than two months. He eventually lost the championship to John Morrison in September 2009 on *SmackDown*.

The loss to John Morrison didn't set Rey Mysterio back for long. Instead, it gave him a stronger desire to be his best. He quickly rebounded with several huge wins over the much bigger Batista before beginning an intense rivalry with CM Punk.

The problems between Mysterio and
Punk began in March 2010 when the
Straight Edge Superstar interrupted a
birthday celebration for Mysterio's
daughter, Aaliyah. Punk's rude actions
helped lead to a series of matches
between the two Superstars.

Mysterio won most of the battles, including a high-profile match at *WrestleMania XXVI*. He also beat Punk at *Over the Limit*. After the match, Mysterio cut off all of Punk's long hair. Punk was greatly angered by his new haircut, but the fans loved it.

Rey Mysterio's success against CM Punk put him right back in the World Championship picture. He competed against Jack Swagger, Big Show, and Punk at the *Fatal 4-Way* pay-per-view. Despite being the smallest Superstar in the ring, he won the match and his second World Championship.

Unfortunately for Mysterio, his second World Title reign was much shorter than his first. Less than one month after capturing the gold,  he lost it to Kane at the *Money in the Bank* pay-per-view. However, as always, Mysterio refused to let the loss get him down. Instead, he went right back to his winning ways, picking up victories over Dolph Ziggler, Drew McIntyre, Jack Swagger, and other top names.

When Rey Mysterio decided to become a Superstar, many believed he was crazy. They told him he was too small.

However, those critics failed to account for the size of Mysterio's heart and his desire to be great. More than 20 years after his first match, the 5' 6" (1.68 m) Superstar has beaten men twice his size on his way to becoming a future Hall of Famer.

Rey Mysterio Facts

• Rey Mysterio's 619 signature move is named after the area code of his hometown, San Diego.

• In the 2006 *Royal Rumble*, Rey Mysterio lasted 1 hour, 2 minutes, and 12 seconds.
No Superstar has ever lasted longer in a *Royal Rumble* match.

• Rey Mysterio has held the WWE Tag Team Championship with Edge, Rob Van Dam, Eddie Guerrero, and Batista.

• Rey Mysterio's entrance theme, "Booyaka 619," is sung by the popular alternative rock band P.O.D.

LONDON, NEW YORK, MUNICH,
MELBOURNE, AND DELHI

For DK/Brady Games
Publisher David Waybright
Editor-in-chief H. Leigh Davis
Licensing Director Mike Degler
International Translations Brian Saliba
Director of Business Development
Michael Vaccaro
Title Manager Tim Fitzpatrick

Reading Consultant
Linda B. Gambrell, Ph.D.

Produced by
Shoreline Publishing Group LLC
President James Buckley Jr.
Designer Tom Carling, carlingdesign.com

For WWE
Director, Home Entertainment & Books
Dean Miller
Photo Department
Frank Vitucci, Joshua Tottenham, Jamie Nelsen,
and Kevin Caldwell
Legal Lauren Dienes-Middlen

First American Edition, 2011
11 12 13 10 9 8 7 6 5 4 3 2 1

Published in the United States by DK Publishing
375 Hudson Street, New York, New York 10014

DK books are available at special discounts when purchased in bulk
for sales promotions, premiums, fund-raising, or educational use.
For details, contact: DK Publishing Special Markets,
375 Hudson Street, New York, New York 10014
SpecialSales@dk.com

A catalog record for this book is available
from the Library of Congress.

ISBN: 978-0-7566-8948-3

Printed and bound by Lake Book.

The publisher would like to thank the following for their kind
permission to reproduce their photographs:
All photos courtesy WWE Entertainment, Inc.
All other images © Dorling Kindersley
For further information see: www.dkimages.com

Discover more at

www.dk.com

John Cena®

Written by Brian Shields

DK

DK Publishing

The scene was *WrestleMania 21*
in 2005. John Cena lifted his
opponent over his head. Then he

slammed WWE Champion JBL to the mat! Cena then landed on top of JBL, pinning his shoulders to the mat. The referee counted—1-2-3! The match was over! John Cena's lifelong dream came true. He was the new WWE Champion!

WWE championships come from hard work and a long journey. Where did John Cena's amazing journey begin?

John Cena grew up in the small town of West Newbury, Massachusetts. As a kid, he loved sports, hip-hop music, and watching WWE. His favorite WWE Superstars were Hulk Hogan, Ultimate Warrior, and Shawn Michaels. He watched their matches on TV.

Hulk Hogan

John dressed in hip-hop fashion.
He loved music, and he made up
his own lyrics and songs about
freedom. Being a young rebel in a
small town wasn't always popular.

He was not liked by
the other kids, who
were more into
hard rock.
They teased
him, which
only made him
more of a rebel.

Shawn Michaels

When Cena turned 15, he found a
new passion. It would stop the
teasing, and it would change his
life forever. He began working out
at the gym and developing himself
as a bodybuilder.

Cena was also a very good student. He applied to 60 colleges and 58 accepted him! He picked Springfield College in Massachusetts.

He made the school's football team as an offensive lineman. He was a Division III All-American and the team's captain. He also earned a degree in exercise physiology (fizz-ee-OHL-oh-jee). He learned more about how the human body works. This helped when he joined WWE.

In 2000, Cena went to California to try a career as a bodybuilder. Competing in WWE was the furthest thing from his mind. He just wanted to build his body.

Then, while working at a gym, he heard about classes at Ultimate Pro Wrestling. Those who did well there could move onto WWE. Cena remembered his WWE heroes.

Cena's Stats and Stuff
- Name: John Cena
- Height: 6'1", Weight: 240 lbs.
- From: Newbury, Mass.
- Finishing Move: "Attitude Adjustment"

He decided to give it a shot. From
the first moment, he was hooked!

Cena learned everything he could about being a WWE Superstar. He quickly moved to the top of his class. Within a year he had caught the eye of WWE officials. They signed him to a contract and sent him to Ohio Valley Wrestling. That's where many future WWE Superstars trained.

At Ohio Valley Wrestling, in 2001, John really learned his stuff.

He impressed his teachers with his body, his strength, and his exciting energy. In June 2002, he took a step he could never have dreamed of as a kid. John Cena became a WWE Superstar.

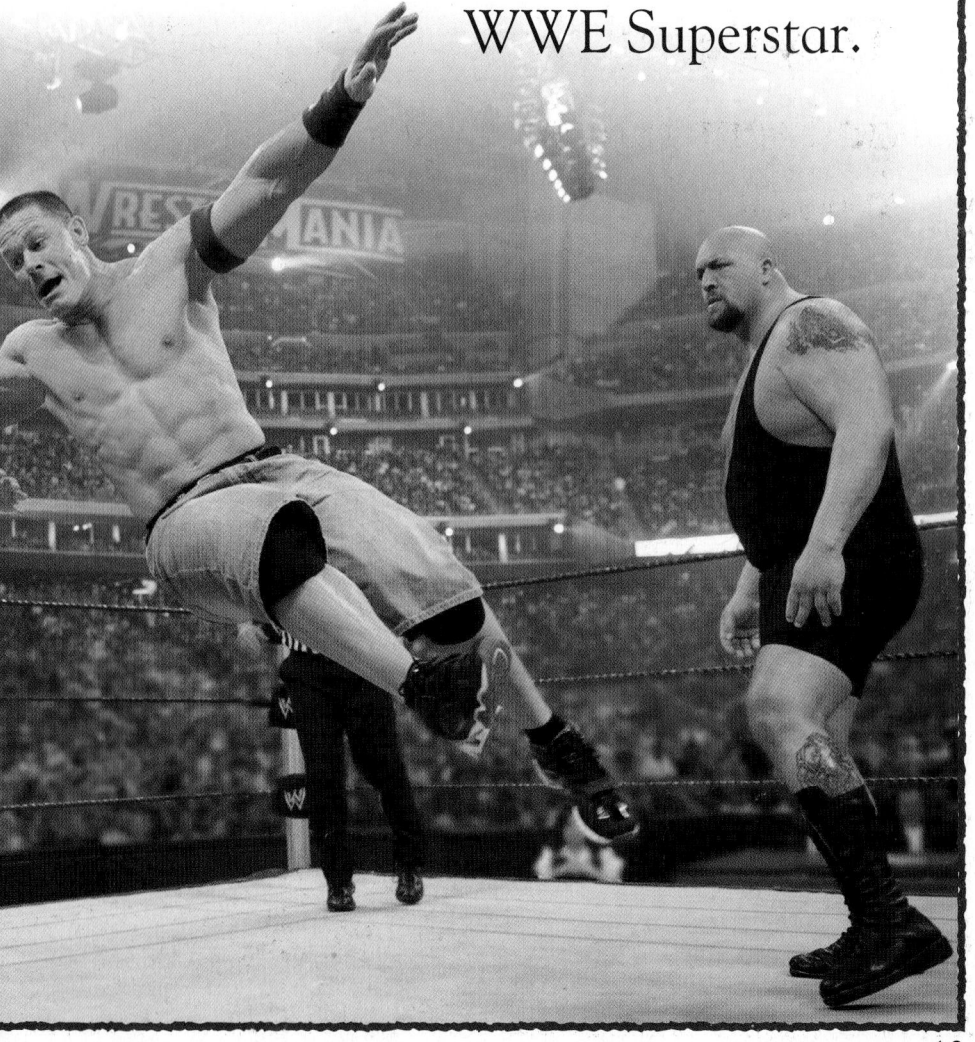

Cena's first WWE matches were on *SmackDown*. His first costume was an old sports jersey and pair of sneakers. His first opponents were Superstars Kurt Angle, Chris

Jericho, Undertaker, Edge, and future WWE Hall-of-Famer Eddie Guerrero.

He picked up the first of his many nicknames. He was called "The Doctor of Thuganomics." He also created several signature moves with colorful names, such as the Attitude Adjustment and the Five-Knuckle Shuffle. Cena would use all of these moves to win!

Cena's first really huge WWE moment came at *WrestleMania XX* in March, 2004. That day he beat the man known as "The World's

Largest Athlete," the 7-foot-tall, 500-pound Big Show. Cena became the WWE United States Champion.

In 2005, he beat JBL at *WrestleMania 21*. That clinched his first WWE Championship. His dream had come true. He had reached the top of the WWE world.

Also in 2005, another dream came true. Cena was part of a tag team with two of his WWE heroes: Shawn Michaels and Hulk Hogan.

Cena spent the first part of
2006 defending his WWE
Championship around the world.
One of his toughest
matches came at
WrestleMania 22

in Chicago. There he battled
Triple H. Cena won with his
patented STF submission hold.

Later that year, Cena lost the title
to Edge, who took him down with
his trademark Spear. Cena had
held the title for 280 days. This
tied him with JBL as the longest
title holder in nearly 20 years.

Cena's WWE Championship History
- 2 World Heavyweight Championships
- 2 World Tag Team Championships
- 3 WWE Championships
- 3 WWE United States Championships
- 2008 *Royal Rumble* Winner

Just three weeks after losing the title, Cena was back on top. He regained the WWE Championship, beating Edge at the *Royal Rumble* in Toronto, Canada.

The two Superstars battled on and off throughout the year. Their toughest match may have been at *Unforgiven 2006.* In a Tables, Ladders & Chairs Match, Cena showed his awesome strength. He tossed Edge off a 16-foot ladder, through two tables! They remain enemies to this day!

With his great success, Cena's
army of fans continued to grow.
His fans began calling themselves
the "Chain Gang." That fan
group earned Cena another
nickname: "The Chain Gang
Commander."

At *WrestleMania 23*, in 2007, Cena took on one of his childhood heroes, WWE legend Shawn Michaels. This famous figure was known as the "Heartbreak Kid" and the "Showstopper."

In a show-stopping move of his own, Cena sped to the match in Detroit in a sleek black Ford  Mustang. Then he defeated Michaels in front of 80,000 screaming fans at

Ford Field to keep his WWE
Championship. After that match,
both Cena and Michaels had
newfound respect for each other.

As his success grew, the list of challengers to Cena's crown kept getting longer. Next up was WWE Superstar Randy Orton. During his battle with Orton, Cena was injured for the first time in his

WWE career. Orton, known as "The Viper," hit Cena with his finishing move, called "the RKO," causing the injury.

Cena was forced to give up his WWE Championship while he recovered from his injury. Healed and rested, John Cena made his return to the ring at the 2008 *Royal Rumble* at Madison Square Garden.

That night, with his Chain Gang rooting him on, Cena took on Triple H. He won the match by throwing Triple H right over the top rope of the WWE ring! The crowd went crazy. "The Champ" was back in the house.

Next up for Cena was the huge celebration of *WrestleMania*'s 25th anniversary in April, 2009.

That night, Cena won his second World Heavyweight Championship. He showed his amazing strength to

win the match. He picked up *both* Big Show and Edge, and slammed them to the mat!

Today, John Cena continues to battle the WWE's most infamous Superstars. Whether he's competing on *Raw* or *SmackDown*, Cena never backs down from a challenge. He never gives up. Superstars like Chris Jericho, The Great Khali, Ted DiBiase, and The Miz have been on the receiving end of Cena's power in the ring.

Cena sometimes teams with his friends, such as Batista,

CM Punk, Rey Mysterio, Cryme Tyme, or Jeff Hardy. But whenever Cena is in the ring, WWE villains must beware of this powerful force of nature.

John Cena is more than just a WWE Superstar. In 2004, Cena was in the *Tribute to the Troops* show. Cena, along with many other WWE Superstars, traveled to the Middle East where they spent time with U.S. soldiers. He also works for the Make-A-Wish Foundation, helping to grant wishes for children with life-threatening illnesses.

Cena released his own rap album and has starred in two movies, *The Marine* and *12 Rounds.*

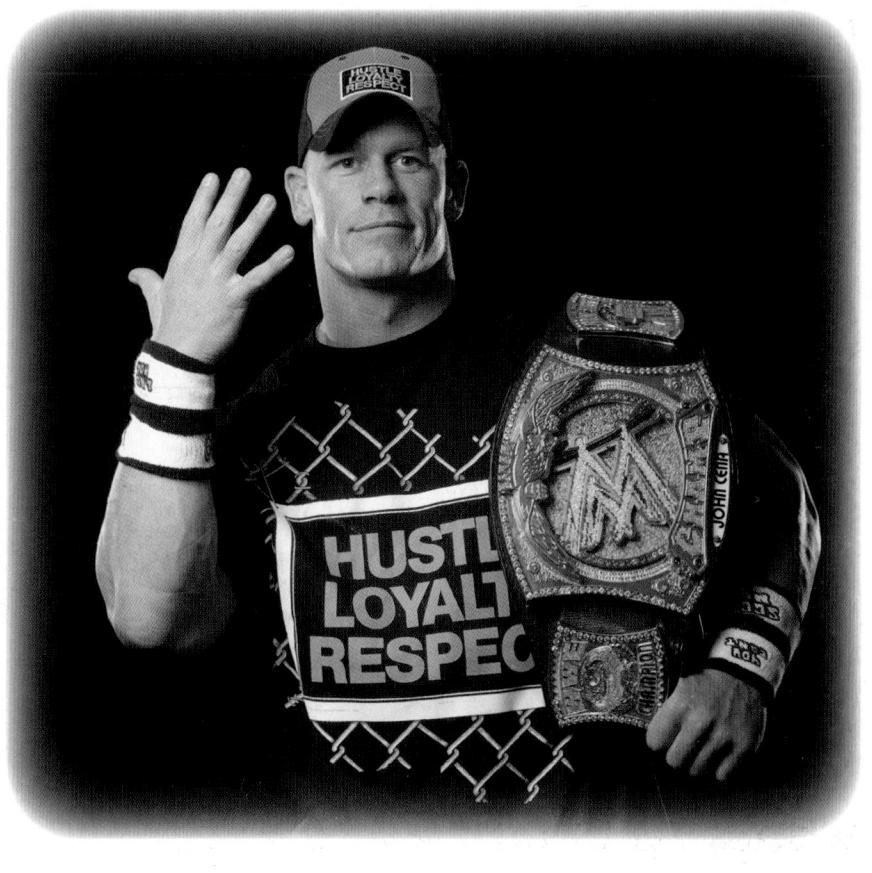

A champion in and out of the ring, John Cena lives by three ideals that have guided him throughout his life: Hustle, Loyalty, and Respect. He's a Superstar any way you look at it.

John Cena Facts

- When John Cena beat WWE Champion JBL at *WrestleMania 21*, he proudly announced, "The Champ is here."

- John Cena's rap album, *You Can't See Me*, hit number 15 on the charts and has sold over 500,000 copies.

- WWE Chairman Vince McMahon once said, "John Cena was born to be WWE Champion."

- A car fan, John Cena's very first car was a 1983 Cadillac Coupe de Ville.